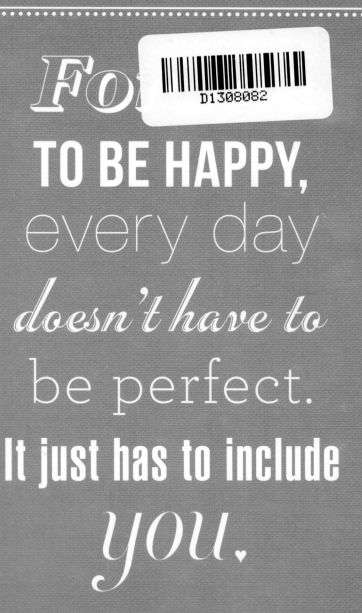

For **TO BE HAPPY,** every day *doesn't have to* be perfect. **It just has to include** *you.*

SMS

I texted to remind you about the groceries.

I called to remind you about the appointment.

I left this note to remind you that

I Love You

(At least you'll remember one out of the three.)

THERE ISN'T ANYONE ELSE I WOULD WANT TO BINGE-WATCH NETFLIX WITH.

ROSES
ARE RED,

THE SUN IS HOT
AND SO ARE YOU.

VIOLETS
ARE BLUE

My records indicate
you're overdue for a massage!
Report home immediately
after work.

Je t'aime

Jeg elsker dig

Mahal Kita

ICH LIEBE DICH

Szeretlek

I love you

Ti amo

AŠ TAVE MYLIU

Amo-te

TECHIHHILA

Seni seviyorum

You. Me.

Tonight.

That moment
when you smile at me
from across the room and
I get all tingly inside.

I love you so much
I bought a license plate
with our names
airbrushed on it.

You're one in a million.

Or, one in 7,248,580,348, to be exact.

What are you thinking about?

Because I'm thinking about

you.

I want us to be

one of those old couples

who sit on a park bench

and hold hands.

You are my

~~BEST FRIEND~~

~~LOVER~~

~~PRINCE~~

~~HERO~~

~~FAVORITE~~

~~PARTNER DESTINY~~

everything.

LET'S
CALL
IN
SICK

AND SPEND THE DAY

together.

YOU'RE

A H⚾MERUN

A TOUCHD🏈WN

A G♥AL

A THREE-POINTER

Game, set, match: me!

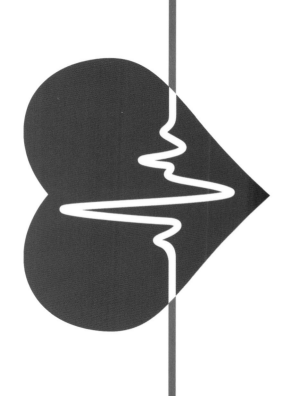

YOU MAKE MY HEART BEAT A LITTLE FASTER.

Our love makes me want to sing some Savage Garden.

Thanks for being
the better half
of our whole.

I love that you know when to refill my wine glass and when to just bring me the whole bottle.

CAN WE BE

US

FOREVER

AND EVER?

THANKS FOR SHARING YOUR

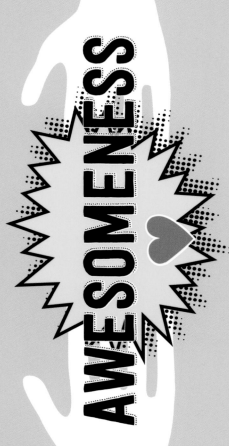

AWESOMENESS

WITH ME.

LET'S FIGHT
SO WE CAN
make up.

You're the last thing
I think of every night
and the first thing
I think of every morning.

HOME IS
WHEREVER
YOU ARE.

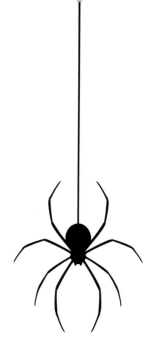

You're the bravest
person I know ...
especially when it comes
to killing spiders.

If you forgive me,
I'LL LET YOU KEEP
THAT HIDEOUS
T-SHIRT FROM
COLLEGE. DEAL?

How did I manage to land the
most wonderful person in the world?

I LOVE YOU MORE THAN ANYTHING IN THE UNIVERSE— EVEN THAT CUTE FORMER PLANET PLUTO.

YOU'RE JUST LIKE
MY FAVORITE
CUP OF COFFEE—
BIG, STRONG,
AND WITH A TOUCH OF
sweetness.